Also by Doug Marlette

The Emperor Has No Clothes
If You Can't Say Something Nice
Drawing Blood
It's a Dirty Job but Somebody Has to Do It
Kudzu
Preacher
Just a Simple Country Preacher
Chocolate Is My Life
There's No Business Like Soul Business
Shred This Book
I Am Not a Televangelist!
Til Stress Do Us Part
A Doublewide with a View
In Your Face
Even White Boys Get the Blues

AMERICAN GOTHIC

DOUG MARLETTE

FAUX BUBBA

Bill and Hillary
Go to Washington

TIMES T BOOKS

RANDOM HOUSE

Published in the United States by Times Books, a
division of Random House, Inc., New York, and
simultaneously in Canada by Random House of
Canada Limited, Toronto.

Library of Congress Cataloging-in-Publication Data

Marlette, Doug
FAUX BUBBA: Bill & Hillary go to Washington/
Doug Marlette.   p.   cm.
ISBN 0-8129-2073-2
1. Presidents—United States—Election, 1992—
Caricatures and cartoons. 2. United States—Politics
and government—1989–1993—Caricatures and
cartoons. 3. Clinton, Bill, 1946–   —Caricatures and
cartoons. 4. American wit and humor, Pictorial.
I. Title.
E884.M37 1993
973.929'0207—dc20   92-56829

Designed by Levavi & Levavi
Manufactured in the United States of America
9 8 7 6 5 4 3 2

For Patricia Blake Hartley,
Artist Mother of Extraordinary Gifts,
with Gratitude

Faux Bubbas

A lot's been said about our new President and Vice President being the Bubba Administration, but as any Southerner can tell you, these guys are hardly Bubbas. Bubbas don't go to Harvard and Yale. If a Bubba ever gave Oxford a second thought, he'd probably think of it as the Ole Miss of England. No, Clinton and Gore are Faux Bubbas—Fake Good Ol' Boys, Counterfeit Crackers, Weekend Billybobs. But one of the reasons it's working for them is because we are living in the age of the Bubba Wannabee. In last year's presidential campaign, we had Ross Perot, the simple country billionaire, and George Bush, the high Wasp preppie with his pork rinds and horseshoes. Plus we're seeing a phenomenal growth of country music, tobacco-chewing Hollywood agents driving Range Rovers down Sunset Boulevard and two-step dancing investment bankers buying pickup trucks and ranches in Montana. The Faux Bubba has straddled the bar stool of America's Achy Breaky Heart.

For years, my comic strip, *Kudzu*, has chronicled the rise of the Faux Bubba, along with the decline of the authentic Good Ol' Boy against the backdrop of the homogenization, gentrification, and urbanization of my native region into something called the Sunbelt. One of my characters, Uncle Dub, runs a service station and shoots buckshot at joggers, and was designated an endangered species by the National Endowment for the Preservation of Indigenous Folk Cultures. He's the last of the Good Ol' Boys, a true Bubba. And if there's one thing he can't stand, it's Faux Bubbas. "Cat hats and blow-dryers don't mix!" he declares defiantly.

Uncle Dub would tell you that there are two kinds of Faux Bubba. Vice President Al Gore's kind represents the more complicated Bubba Wannabees, like George Bush and Ross Perot. Born to wealth and privilege, refinement and the perks of civilization, they don the bib-overall persona, the rustic coloration and plumage of the Good Ol' Boy as a kind of camouflage to disguise their advantages. They are shrewd politicians who know that Americans root for the underdog and can be as unforgiving of life's winners as they can be of its losers.

In this way, the Bush, Gore, and Perot brand of Faux Bubba is closer to the yuppie novelists, actors, news anchors, and Wall Street brokers flocking to buy ranches in Montana and Wyoming, drive Range Rovers, and go white-water canoeing. This kind of Bubba pose is a testosterone thing. Bridling under the demands of civilization, battered by the women's movement, longing for tribal identity, but too proud to beat drums and weep openly at seminars, they are restoring their masculinity the only way they know how—by buying it. This Faux Bubba life-style has all the perks and bennies, like dipping snuff and chewing tobacco, with none of the cultural downside, like getting laid off from your job or cut up in a knife fight.

Bill Clinton may not be a true Bubba, but he is a true redneck; like me he is just a generation or two removed from the mill villages and trailer parks, trying to assimilate like the children of immigrants, glossing over his ethnicity and trying to "pass" in the predominant culture. Clinton never knew his real daddy, who was killed in a car wreck. His mama's been married five times to four men and she's buried three of them. His stepdaddy was a drunk, his brother went to prison. Hell, Bill Cinton's life *is* a country song.

His grandfather ran a small grocery store in Arkansas, and my grandparents were Carolina textile workers (called lintheads back then). By the grace of Adolf Hitler, my father escaped the mills. I was a military brat, raised in small towns across the South —some of them so backward even the Episcopalians handled snakes. Clinton and I grew up on the historical fault line between the old Confederacy and the New South, between Dixie and the Sunbelt. As Southerners, we are defined as much by our pasts as our present, as much by where we came from as by where we are going.

We grew up in a time and place when it cost you something to be right on race and to question the war in Vietnam. For our generation of young Southerners, going against the grain in a part of the country where white supremacy and military supremacy were articles of faith was a gut-wrenching rite of passage that turned us inside out, defined us morally and made us who we are today. We weren't spoon-fed our values and ideals; we had to earn them. They are not just in our brains now—they're in our bones.

The modern media age and the synthetic mass culture waged war on our Bubba genes. They were stalked and assaulted, educated and refined, gentrified and upwardly mobilized into submission. But the final skirmishes of Antietam and Gettysburg,

Chickamauga and Chancellorsville are still being fought on the battlefields of our souls.

We're still recognizable, though. We're the ones with the designer bib overalls and the gunracks in our BMWs. We sometimes confuse sushi with bait, and we sip our Evian from an old mason jar. Brought up on grits and barbecue, we now make our own pasta and dine on soyburger and calamari. No matter how hard we try, we still can't use "summer" as a verb, and when we say "ciao," we really mean "Ya'll come and see us now, y'heah."

But as Clinton has seen—and will see for the next four or more years—being a Bubba in today's world can be risky. In this age of political correctness, we white, male, heterosexual Southerners represent everything that is wrong with the twentieth century. We are white when black is beautiful, male when sisterhood is powerful, straight when gay is good. We're the wrong color, the wrong race, the wrong sexual orientation, and we speak with the wrong accent. A recent National Opinion Research Center survey compared the images of the five ethnic groups—Jews, blacks, Asians, Hispanics, and white Southerners—and found that white Southerners were perceived as dumber, lazier, and more prone to violence than "white Americans." We didn't need a poll to tell us that. Anti-Southern bias is always lurking below the surface in the national media. Hollywood knows that if you want to make someone a villain or a dimwit, all you have to do is give them a Southern accent. We learn the codes of Northern intolerance the way blacks learn to decipher and interpret the codes of racism. The malign Morse by which it is communicated ("... and you know, Clinton is smart too!") is as recognizable to us as the phrases "welfare chiselers" or "articulate black man" are to African-Americans.

But as Senator Sam Ervin proved during the Senate Watergate hearings, there are advantages to being condescended to and underestimated. Ol' Slick Willie must have been aware of the unconscious bigotry against white Southerners when he selected another Bubba-American as his running mate, because he sure made it work for him. By stacking the ticket with Southerners, he changed the question on everybody's mind from "Did he commit adultery?" to "Has he committed incest?" The answer is no and Clinton is the forty-second President of the United States. Slick, all right. And he sho'nuff didn't learn that at Yale.

REDNECK CHIC (WEEKEND BILLYBOBS)

HOW TO DISTINGUISH THE *REAL* THING FROM *BUBBA WANNABEES*:

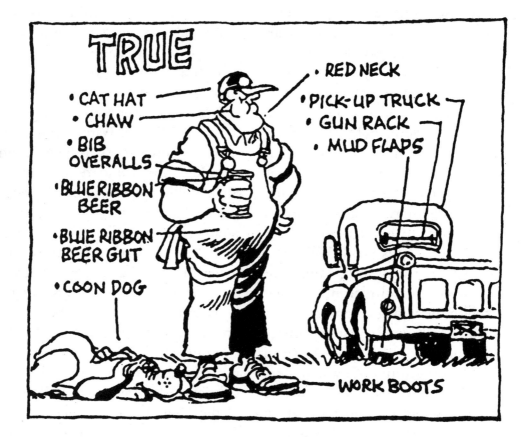

DEFINING FAUX MOMENT:

YOUNG BILL IN GRANDFATHER'S COUNTRY STORE,

DEFINING FAUX MOMENT:

BILL DECIDES TO PLAY SAXOPHONE
INSTEAD OF BANJO.

DEFINING FAUX MOMENT:

IN SHOP CLASS BILL MAKES
CRUDE *ROLODEX*

DEFINING FAUX MOMENT:

BILL READS WELFARE REFORM PROPOSALS TO
HILLARY ON FIRST DATE AT YALE LAW

FAUX BUBBA FOLLIES

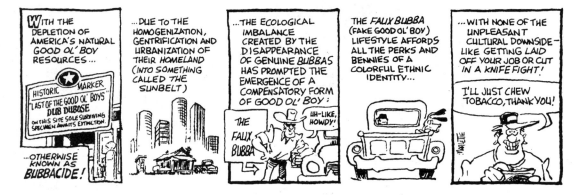

BILL AND HILLARY ANNOUNCING CANDIDACY

"CLINTON'S GETTING COCKY!"

"I LIKE *BUCHANAN'S* SOUND BITES, BUT *CLINTON* AND *TSONGAS* HAVE SLICKER PRODUCTION VALUES!"

"WELCOME TO THE NEXT DEMOCRATIC DEBATE!..."

"WE'RE LAGGING IN THE POLLS, THE CAMPAIGN'S STALLED, BROWN WON'T GO AWAY, THE MEDIA IGNORE US!... OH, WELL, AT LEAST THINGS CAN'T GET ANY WORSE, RIGHT, HILLARY?!..."

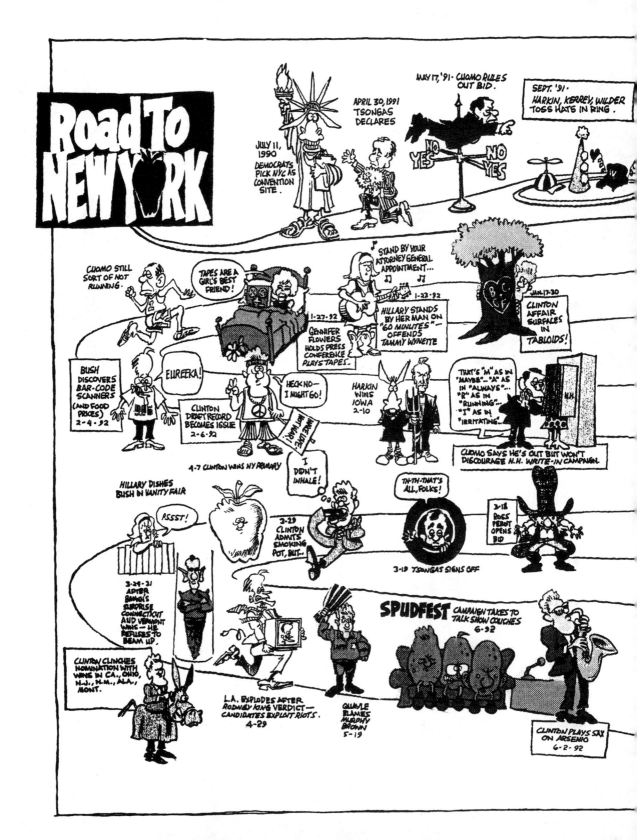

CLINTON TAKES MANHATTAN

MADISON SQ. GARDEN

I ♥ NY

THE *DREAM TEAM*

"YOU CAN SIT DOWN NOW, MARIO!... "

CONVENTION SKETCHBOOK

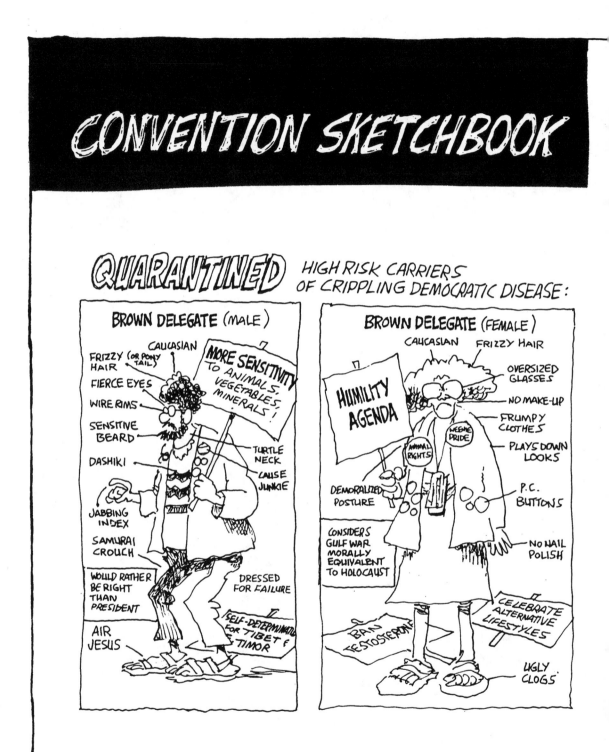

TELL-TALE SYMPTOMS*

- SMUG SELF-RIGHTEOUSNESS
- IDENTIFICATION ONLY WITH VICTIMS
- HOLIER-THAN-THOU ATTITUDE
- PERENNIAL OUTSIDER
- UNCOMFORTABLE WITH WINNING
- GUILT OVER AGGRESSION
- PRIDE IN *PASSIVE* AGGRESSION
- DEFEAT CONSIDERED SOMEHOW VIRTUOUS.

ISOLATED BACILLI

VIRUS MAGNIFIED 20,000 X

* *VIRUS STARTS IN THE BLEEDING HEART AND GOES STRAIGHT FOR THE BRAIN!*

CONVENTION SKETCHBOOK

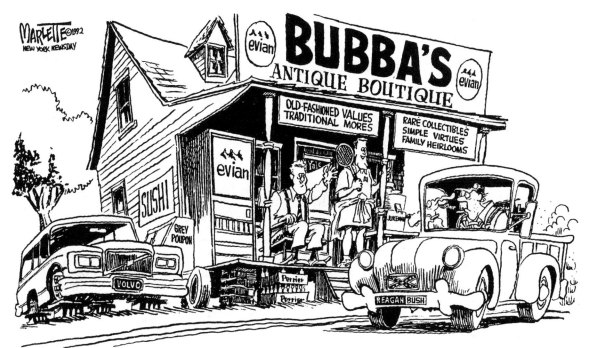

"Y'ALL COME SEE US NOW, Y'HEAH?!"

" HELLO, BAKER ?... ABOUT THESE NEW SETTLEMENTS IN OUR OCCUPIED TERRITORIES !... "

DRAWING ON THE UPPER WEST SIDE OF THE BRAIN...

HOW TO CARICATURE LIBERAL DEMOCRATS

DUELING JAWBONES
THE CLINTON-GORE TICKET—THEY BOTH HAVE THAT *DUDLEY DO-RIGHT* JAWLINE...

TED KENNEDY FEATURES SQUINCHED INTO MIDDLE OF FACE!

WITH HIS PROMINENT NOSE, BROWS, BURNS AND RECEDING HAIRLINE *JERRY BROWN* LOOKS LIKE A WASHED-UP VULTURE!

JESSE JACKSON'S HEAD LOOKS LIKE A BOMB!

MARLETTE NYC 1992

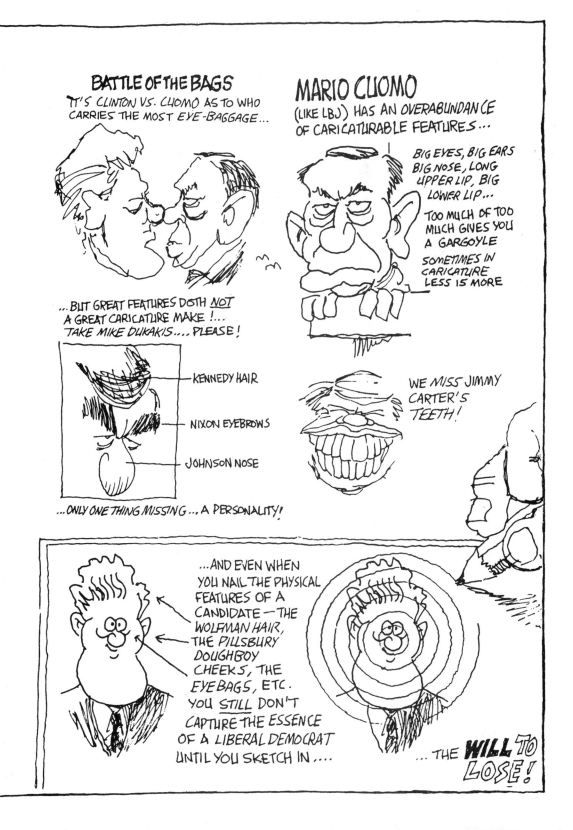

BATTLE OF THE BAGS

IT'S CLINTON VS. CUOMO AS TO WHO CARRIES THE MOST *EYE-BAGGAGE*...

MARIO CUOMO

(LIKE LBJ) HAS AN OVERABUNDANCE OF CARICATURABLE FEATURES...

BIG EYES, BIG EARS BIG NOSE, LONG UPPER LIP, BIG LOWER LIP...

TOO MUCH OF TOO MUCH GIVES YOU A GARGOYLE

SOMETIMES IN CARICATURE LESS IS MORE

...BUT GREAT FEATURES DOTH <u>NOT</u> A GREAT CARICATURE MAKE !... TAKE MIKE DUKAKIS.... PLEASE !

KENNEDY HAIR

NIXON EYEBROWS

JOHNSON NOSE

WE *MISS* JIMMY CARTER'S *TEETH!*

...ONLY ONE THING MISSING... A PERSONALITY!

...AND EVEN WHEN YOU NAIL THE PHYSICAL FEATURES OF A CANDIDATE — THE *WOLFMAN HAIR*, THE *PILLSBURY DOUGHBOY CHEEKS*, THE *EYE BAGS*, ETC. YOU <u>STILL</u> DON'T CAPTURE THE ESSENCE OF A *LIBERAL DEMOCRAT* UNTIL YOU SKETCH IN ....

... THE **WILL TO LOSE!**

"...AND DO YOU, BILL CLINTON, TAKE THIS WOMAN TO BE YOUR LAWFUL, WEDDED WIFE?...."

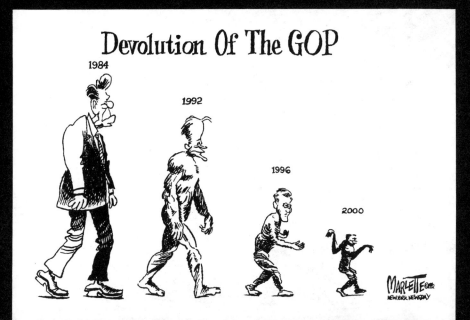

"THIS TOWN AIN'T BIG ENOUGH FOR *BOTH* OF US, PODNUH!"

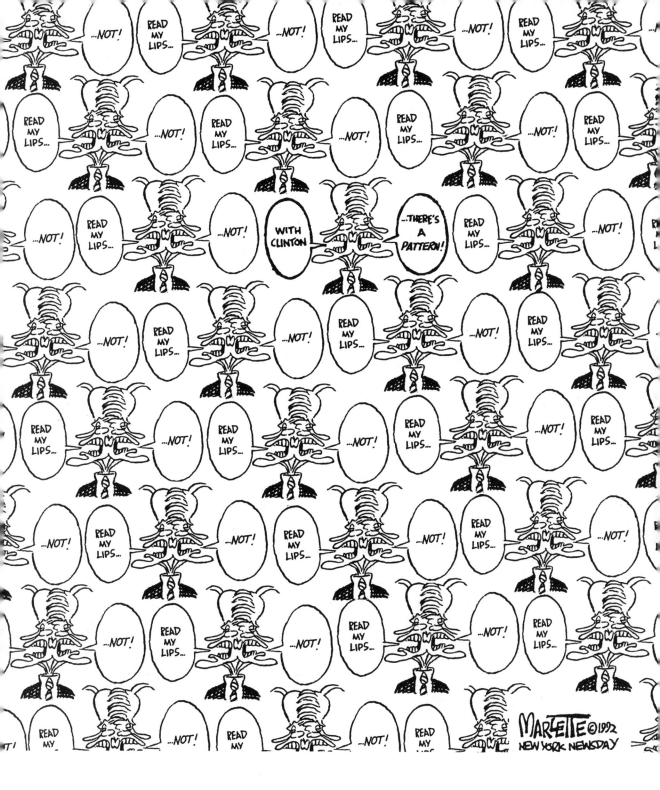

"CAN QUAYLE'S DAD PULL SOME STRINGS?!..."

" MIND IF WE PLAY THROUGH ?! "

" HE'S JUST *CHANNEL-GRAZING* FOR A *POLL* HE LIKES!"

"MORE GOOD NEWS—QUAYLE DIDN'T DROOL ON HIMSELF!"

"I DON'T CARE WHAT THE POLLS SAY, GEORGE—YOU'RE STILL ON THE TICKET!"

WE ALL HAVE OUR *ROSS TO BEAR*

" ...AND FILLING IN FOR JAY LENO THIS WEEK IS *H. ROSS PEROT!...* "

PEROT

TEXAS LONGHORN

" *EARNED* IT ?... NO, HE JUST *BOUGHT* IT ! "

"SORRY, MIKE WALLACE, WE HAVE TO PUT YOU ON HOLD!...WE'VE GOT *DAN RATHER*, *BARBARA WALTERS*, *TOM BROKAW* AND *TED KOPPEL* ON CALL-WAITING, BUT FIRST A FAX FROM *KATIE COURIC* AND A FOLLOW-UP FAX FROM *PETER JENNINGS!...*"

"...ON THE OTHER HAND, JUST BECAUSE YOU'RE PARANOID DOESN'T MEAN THE BUSH CAMPAIGN IS *NOT* OUT TO GET YOU!"

RoosevElvis

POLLS

CLINTON

MARLETTE ©1992
NEW YORK NEWSDAY

" WELCOME TO 'MEET THE PRESS'! "

BILL CLINTON CAMPAIGNS FOR THE COVETED *DUB DUBOSE* VOTE :

LET ME TAKE A MOMENT TO EXPLAIN MY SMALL FILLIN' STATION OWNER SUBSIDY PLAN ...

LATER...

...AND THE SAVINGS WOULD BE PLOWED BACK INTO THE HEALTH-CARE PLAN ALONG WITH THE PEACE DIVIDEND AND MY DAUGHTER CHELSEA'S ALLOWANCE.

SECRETARY OF BARBECUE! HOW DOES THAT SOUND?

"JUST HANG ON—BAKER WILL BE HERE SOON!"

"THAT'S RIGHT, PETER — ACCORDING TO OUR EXIT POLLS THE MOOD OF THE VOTERS THIS YEAR IS ANGRY!"

WHICH CARD IS GEORGE BUSH NOW TRYING TO RUN UP THE NATIONAL DEBT ON?

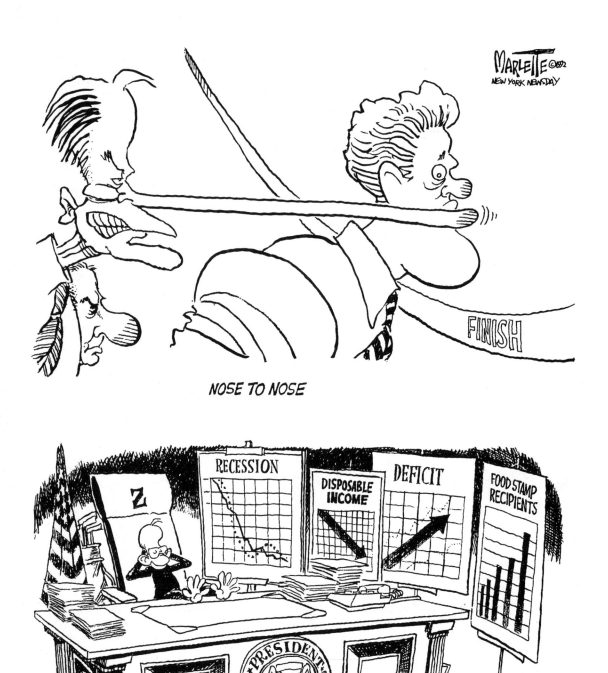

NOSE TO NOSE

UNCURIOUS GEORGE

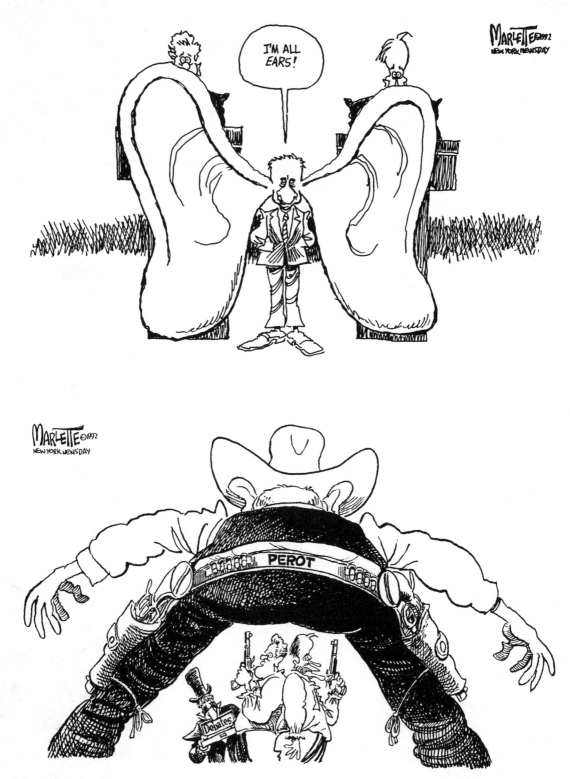

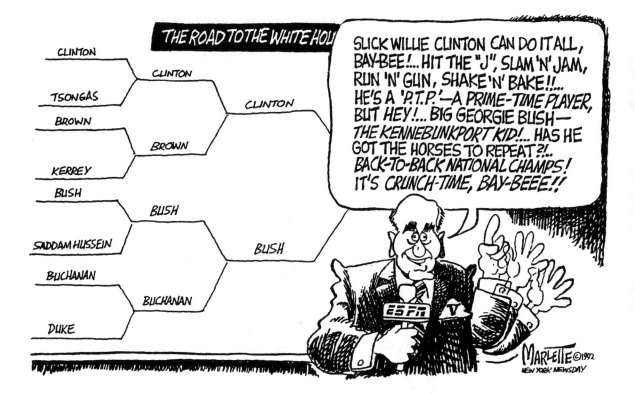

My Son, the Republican

Jackson Marlette is five years old. When he sensed that his mother and I were not exactly pulling for the president of the United States to win reelection, he was confused. "Why, Daddy? Why don't you want President Bush to win?" he asked at first, peering earnestly up at me with blue-eyed, towheaded innocence.

Whenever the President appeared on the news and we seemed less than enthusiastic, hooting and hissing and generally expressing disrespect for the commander in chief, Jackson was perplexed. Then as the campaign went on, he got annoyed. Unfamiliar with the notion of a loyal opposition, the vigorousness of a two-party system, or the electoral vicissitudes of participatory democracy, Jackson thought this kind of dissent was downright treasonous. "Face it," I told my wife, "we're raising a Republican."

Like most boys his age, Jackson admires superheroes like Batman, Superman, the Flash, and Robin Hood, just as I had when I was his age. But Jackson's adulation extends to an even stranger array of contemporary demigods as well—like Teenage

Mutant Ninja Turtles and the Terminator, Wolverine and Hulk Hogan of the World Wrestling Federation. The rule for inclusion in his personal pantheon seems to be: If you have muscles and inordinate strength and personal power, Jackson is in your corner. So I guess I shouldn't

have been surprised when my son declared himself early on for George Bush. After all, Bush was the President, The Head Honcho, the man Jackson was old enough to remember facing down Saddam Hussein on TV. George Bush had muscle, George Bush had the weapons, George Bush was Jackson's man.

When Bill Clinton won his party's nomination, and it became clear that Clinton was the candidate of choice of his mother and father, Jackson couldn't believe it. It was as if his parents were pulling for the Joker, or Shredder, or Skeletor, or the Sheriff of Nottingham. How could we not support the commander in chief? "I'm for Bush, Dad," he would announce after a commercial for the reelection of the president. "Are you for Bush, Dad? He's the President, Dad. Aren't you for the President?"

As the campaign rolled into the fall, heating up with campaign spots and talk-show appearances and news coverage, Jackson saw his parents glued to the TV with our allegiances on our sleeves. Slowly, his annoyance blossomed into belligerence. The debates got him really ticked. His support of the President was as firm and immutable as Dan Quayle's. If Bush had shown as much enthusiasm for his own candidacy as Jackson did, he might still be in the White House.

In late October, a week before the election, word spread around the little North Carolina town of Hillsborough, where we have a home, that the Clinton-Gore bus tour was coming our way. Jackson and his classmates were let out of school early for the rally, which was being held at the courthouse, a couple of yards from our front door. As the town square filled up with people, Jackson, wearing his OshKosh B'Gosh overalls, crouched on the curb in the afternoon sun. We explained that the crowd was there to see Bill Clinton and Al Gore, possibly the next President and Vice-President of the United States. Jackson was unimpressed. When the Clinton-Gore buses finally rolled up two hours late and the throng surged, Jackson sat still, unenthusiastic. During the speeches, Jackson was blasé. But then, when Clinton finally made his way around the courthouse square and came toward Jackson's mother and me in the crowd, I picked up Jackson so he could shake hands with Clinton. We ended up being hugged by the candidate, making a Jackson sandwich, with our son squeezed between my wife, Bill Clinton, and me. Jackson was actually hugged by the next President of the United States, the man he had watched on TV for so long, just like Batman.

As the buses rolled out of Hillsborough, heading on to the next town, and the crowd broke up and drifted away, we walked back home, flushed with energy and excitement. Jackson trotted alongside his chattering parents, holding my hand and balancing on the curb, head down, saying very little. Finally he looked up at me and said brightly, "Y'know, Dad...I think I'll vote for Clinton now."

Jackson's support for Clinton never wavered through the following week. My wife and I thought we were keeping our delight at his conversion to ourselves, but it was hard to hide. Then, just the night before the election, I was telling Jackson a bedtime story and tucking him in when, out of the blue, he decided, "Daddy, maybe it'll be a tie."

"What's that, son?" I asked.

"For President. Maybe Bush and Clinton and Perot will tie. Then everybody will win. Nobody will lose."

"I don't think so, Jackson," I explained. "I'm afraid somebody has to win and somebody has to lose."

"Not this time, Dad," he insisted. "They're going to tie. I know it."

Bill Clinton won the election, and Jackson seemed to accept with equanimity the fact that Clinton didn't have to share his victory with Bush and Perot. Nothing much was discussed about the election results in the days that followed. But a couple of weeks later, we were eating dinner at a local restaurant, and as it turned out, Jackson was not on his best behavior. If politicians can have a bad hair day, my son was having a bad attitude day. All afternoon he had been sullen, defiant, sassy, and incorrigible. He was not eating his meal, fidgeting and interrupting our conversation, and generally disturbing the ambiance the owners of the restaurant have strived so successfully to create. All attempts at negotiation fell on deaf ears. So did pleading, wheedling, threats, and bribery— nothing worked.

When he started getting up out of his seat and roaming the restaurant, harassing the other diners instead of finishing his pasta, his mother and I reached the end of our patience. "That's it," I growled to my wife. "You pay for the meal. I'm taking Jackson out to the car. We're going home and he's going straight to bed." I marched him down the stairs and out the door. In the car, we sat waiting in icy silence with me behind the wheel and Jackson in the back seat. We were both seething. Nothing was said between us for several minutes as we waited for my wife to finish her meal and pay the bill. Finally, the quiet was broken by Jackson's voice.

"Dad," he said fiercely.

"What?"

"I'm not voting for Clinton now."

"I INHALED!"

BABY BOOMER-IN-CHIEF

" JUST MORE *BILLS.!...* "

BOATLOADS OF *LIBERALS,* ADRIFT FOR YEARS AS POLITICAL REFUGEES, WERE INTERCEPTED BY THE COAST GUARD TODAY AS THEY MADE THEIR WAY UP THE POTOMAC SEEKING ASYLUM IN *BILL CLINTON'S AMERICA...*

91

" WHAT YOU MEAN 'WE', KEMO SABE ?!... "

"EXPECT NO MIRACLES!"

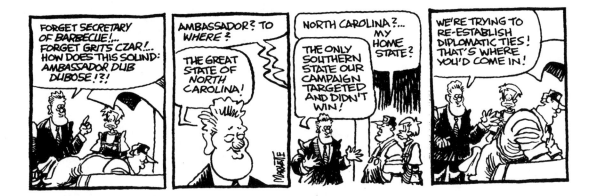

"...AND ROLLER BLADES, AND A BARBIE DREAM HOUSE, AND HILLARY FOR ATTORNEY GENERAL!..."

LET ME GET THIS STRAIGHT—YOU WANT TO APPOINT ME AMBASSADOR TO THE STATE OF NORTH CAROLINA?!

WE LOST THE STATE—NO NEED TO BURN BRIDGES!

IT MAKES SENSE—YOU'RE A NATIVE... YOU SPEAK THEIR LANGUAGE... YOU ALREADY LIVE THERE, SO THERE'S NO PAPERWORK!...

OF COURSE, THERE ARE RISKS: TWO REPUBLICAN SENATORS... JESSE HELMS COUNTRY...

YOU COULD BE TAKEN HOSTAGE—LET'S NOT SUGARCOAT IT!

YOU DON'T WANT TO BE AMBASSADOR TO NORTH CAROLINA, SECRETARY OF BARBECUE, OR GRITS CZAR?...

...THEN WHAT ON EARTH DO YOU WANT FROM ME?!

NOTHING!

FACE IT, SIR—WE DO HAVE A PERSON TO WASTE!

No, Virginia, there is no Santa Claus... However, there is an uptick in the latest consumer confidence index!

THE TORCH IS PASSED TO A *NEW GENERATION*

Close Encounters of the Presidential Kind

People say that cartoonists have a love/hate relationship with politicians, but the truth is, we love to hate 'em. Not personally, but professionally. A good cartoonist is a semiautomatic assault weapon. And we are only as good as our targets are bad. And ugly.

We thrive on corruption and sleaze. We look at national trauma the way a plastic surgeon looks at crow's-feet or cellulite. It's too bad, but hey, it's a living.

Ronald Reagan was heaven for us. Drawing cartoons during those years was like shooting fish in a barrel. George Bush was also a dream—if only because he gave us Dan Quayle. Bill Clinton, on the other hand, is a problem. As a cartoonist, it isn't easy to admit but, I . . . I kinda like Bill Clinton. There, I've said it. I'm not exactly saying he is a FOD (Friend of Doug), but he is the first President I've drawn with whom I actually feel some personal connection. Clinton is a fellow left-hander, a fellow Southerner, and a fellow yuppie. In other words, a Faux Bubba like me. I not only share Bill Clinton's and Al Gore's accents, I even share their religious upbringings—Southern Baptist. Bill, Al, and I grew up singing the same hymns, espousing the same theology ("A dancin' foot and a prayin' knee don't grow on the same laig") and drinking the same Welch's communion grape juice. As a citizen, I was pleased with the election results, but as a cartoonist I am profoundly depressed. Give me a Richard Nixon or a Jesse Helms any day.

I usually try to avoid meeting politicians. I know I might gain some first-hand knowledge of caricaturable physiognomy, but it doesn't make up for potential damage that could occur to my professional radar. I'll work from photographs, thanks. After all, even the most heinous public servants have wives and kids, as well as dogs they are kind to. Meeting politicians carries with it the risk—however marginal—that I might find them charming, engaging, or personally decent. And if that happens, how am I supposed to ridicule such a fine person? But, as we all know, a politician's personal qualities have nothing to do with how well he or she serves the public. Genghis Khan may have been Mr. Charisma, but tell that to the Tartars he carved up.

It doesn't help that nowadays we get to know so much about public figures. Not only do we hear their confessions on Phil and Oprah and Larry King, but we see interviews with their shrinks and proctologists. Personally, I'm glad I don't know that Benedict Arnold raised geraniums or that Joseph Goebbels kept a butterfly collection. I don't care that Saddam Hussein watches CNN or enjoys "Gilligan's Island" reruns. Such tidbits humanize these despots and psychos. Empathy may be all right for the novelist or psychoanalyst, but it's deadly for a cartoonist. When you start identifying with your targets, you lose the killer instinct and cartoons become oatmeal.

Don't get me wrong. I'm not a fanatic about avoiding politicians. I just don't go out of my way to meet them. Somehow I suspect the feeling is mutual. "What wart is he seeing?" they wonder. "What hideous physical defect is he noticing?" (This is actually a great myth about cartoonists. We don't see caricatures everywhere we look, any more than dentists see truant flossers and overbites or shrinks see manic-depressives and borderline schizophrenics. We keep it in the office.) I have not been exactly flood-ed over the years with invitations to dine with politicians. Dan Quayle seldom thinks of me when putting together a golf foursome. Mario Cuomo doesn't call me up and say, "Pick up a pizza and a six-pack and come over to watch the Knicks on TV."

When you go around pointing out the emperor's nekkidness, he's not likely to invite you to join the volleyball game at the nudist colony.

Still, when I met Bill Clinton several years ago, I wasn't too concerned about protecting my professional radar. I lived in North Carolina and he was the governor of Arkansas, so there wasn't much chance that I'd ever draw him. And anyway, the time I met Jesse Helms he was a perfect gentleman, and that didn't stop me from ravaging him in my cartoons. I'd felt affection for Jimmy Carter, but you couldn't tell it in my work.

I first ran into Clinton at Hilton Head, South Carolina, at the Renaissance Weekend, the now famous yuppie networking retreat for politicos and corporate and media types, which has been credited with helping launch his candidacy for president This weekend is full of golf and tennis, but mainly consists of informal seminars and chats about everything from "Something That's Been Bugging Me Lately" to "The Tumor on the Soul of America." This was also my first time hearing Clinton speak. He was riveting, dynamic and engaging, and he exhibited more intelligence, depth and breadth, and vision than I had ever seen before in a politican. "He's going to run for President someday," I commented to my wife. "And he should." I kept my concern over having to draw someone I liked in check until he announced for the presidency. Still, he was one of several wannabees, and from where I sat his chances looked slim. But as the campaign wore on and I was naturally called upon to draw him more and more, the old problems arose again.

The great cartoonist Bill Mauldin once confessed that he thought his caricature of Jack Kennedy was compromised because he liked Kennedy so much. When I drew cartoons in Atlanta, I struggled with my caricature of Mayor Andy Young for the same reasons—not because he was especially tricky to draw, but due to my basic respect for him. Whenever I started to sketch him, I had a tendency to choke. The caricature was tight and inhibited, more like an official portrait. The cartoonist's art is as subjective as anything else, but to serve the truth in what we do, our drawings have to rely on an instinctual objectivity that leads sometimes to viciousness and cruelty.

Sure enough, my early Clintons were restrained—the first warning signs of a cartoonist's affection for his target. I was choking. Fortunately, along came Gennifer Flowers and the draft revelations. My Clinton caricature loosened up during the New Hampshire primary—he began to look goofier, more out of control. As his troubles increased, my drawings became better. His junk food pudginess helped. By the New York primary, I was rolling. Hillary was a little easier. Men are usually easier to draw because of the harder, more angular features; women are more of a challenge—especially pretty ones like Hillary. The headband helped. But while Bill's personal warmth interfered with my professional radar, Hillary's coolness was an asset. Bill was a hugger, his wife shook hands. The dangers were all brought home to me again at the annual Renaissance get-together just before the inauguration, when my worst nightmare came true. Art Buchwald and I had been commiserating about what a problem a likable Clinton was for satirists. We were headed for the bar when we passed the President-elect surrounded by a gaggle of well-wishers. Clinton grabbed my arm for a word. Buchwald made it to the bar and ordered drinks.

"Where's Marlette?" he asked.

"He's being hugged by the President," someone told him.

Buchwald repeated this story with great glee. My feeble protests of "I didn't hug him—he hugged me" sounded pitiful. We both agreed that if word got out that a political cartoonist had been hugged by the President, he could get drummed out of the cartoonists' coven, medals and ribbons stripped and Pulitzer rescinded. Buchwald confided, "Y'know, I saw Clinton at a party last night and I must say"—he glanced over his shoulder guiltily as if confessing a morals charge —"he was very nice to me."

"I know what you mean," I replied. "Every time he hugs me, I go up to my room and tear up two or three nasty cartoons."

I'm not saying a likable Clinton is a disaster for cartoonists. The jogging, the Big Mac attacks, Socks the cat: they're all helpful, but not really enough. If he wanted to make our jobs a lot easier, he would exchange arms for hostages, obstruct justice, or lie under oath to Congress. Or at the very least, go back to the hairdo he had at Oxford, the one that looked like it was styled by Cuisinart.

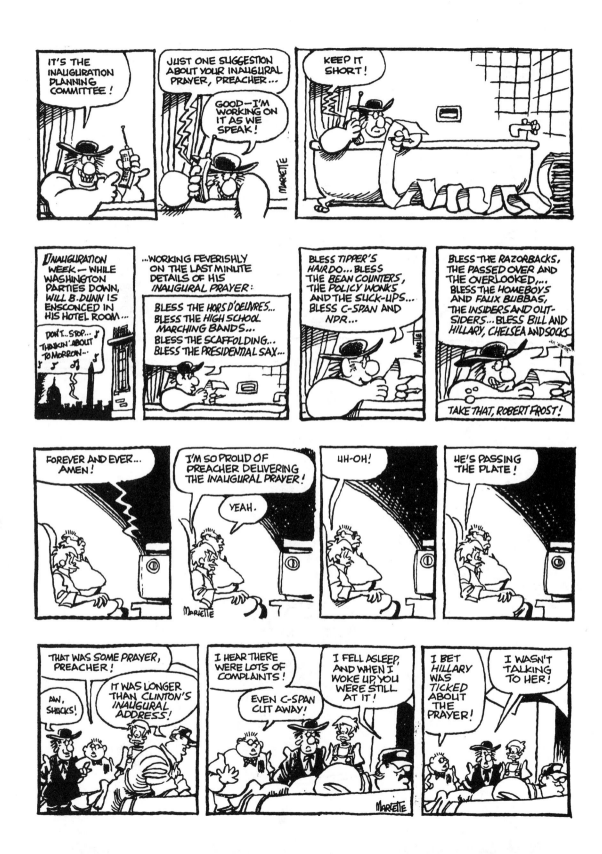

" NO, HILLARY ! "

"... DO YOU, BILL CLINTON, PROMISE TO PRESERVE, PROTECT AND DEFEND THE CONSTITUTION OF THE UNITED STATES AND SWEAR YOU'LL NEVER PLAY *FLEETWOOD MAC'S* 'DON'T STOP THINKING ABOUT TOMORROW' *EVER AGAIN* ?!... "

IF THE CLINTONS WERE *REAL* BUBBAS...

CHELSEA AND SOCKS

FIRST FELINE

FIRST KITTY
LITTER

FIRST
HAIR
BALL

OUT OF THE CLOSET

OVAL OFFICE AGING PROCESS

THE NEW PRESIDENT JOGGING

SOCKS' SECURITY

"NEVER MIND YOUR LAW ENFORCEMENT EXPERIENCE — DID YOU EVER HIRE AN *ILLEGAL ALIEN?!...*"

"GRENADA... PANAMA... PERSIAN GULF... AND THIS ONE FOR BASHING GAYS IN SAN DIEGO!..."

About the Author

DOUG MARLETTE won the 1988 Pulitzer Prize for editorial cartooning and is the only cartoonist to have received a Nieman Fellowship at Harvard. He currently draws for *New York Newsday*, and his work is regularly reprinted in *The New York Times*, *Newsweek*, and *The Washington Post*. Twelve collections of his cartoons have been published, among them *In Your Face: A Cartoonist at Work* and *Even White Boys Get the Blues*.